Natalie

BY ROBERT DUMONT

**NATALIE JACKSON: VOICES & FRAGMENTS
A BIOGRAPHICAL COLLAGE**

ROSACE
Publications

Copyright © 2025 by Robert Dumont

Published in the United States by
Rosace Publications
www.rosacepublications.com

Book Design: Astra Beck

Cover Photograph:
By Allen Ginsberg, featuring Natalie Jackson,
Neal Cassady, and Peter Du Peru

Interior Photographs (pp. 12, 26, and 44):
Photographs by Allen Ginsberg, provided courtesy of
Peter Hale, Executor of the Allen Ginsberg Estate

Image on page 22:
San Francisco Chronicle, Thursday, December 1, 1955

All rights reserved. No part of this publication may be reproduced, stored in a retrieval system, or transmitted in any form or by any means—electronic, mechanical, photocopying, recording, or otherwise—without prior written permission from the publisher.

Cataloging-in-Publication Data is available from
the Library of Congress.

Library of Congress Control Number: 2025907084
ISBN (Paperback): 978-0-9997777-3-2

First Edition, June 2025
Printed in the United States of America

CONTENTS

AUTHOR'S NOTE vii

PART 01 1

PART 02 7

PART 03 13

PART 04 23

PART 05 27

PART 06 33

PART 07 37

PART 08 41

CODA 45

FROM THE LENS OF ALLEN GINSBERG 48

BIBLIOGRAPHY 49

ABOUT THE AUTHOR 51

PRAISES FOR NATALIE

"As someone who had not previously known of Natalie Jackson or her story, I was delighted to find this book. It's both a great introduction and a sideways glance through a window into the world of the Beats—a time and a place and people who ate and drank and wrote and f..... inally did a lot of other things. The collage method employed by the author was the right call to make. There are life-story gaps in everyone's life and in this case the tragic narrative makes a poignant virtue of them. Our imaginations are thus invited to connect the dots."

RYAN PETTY
Author of the forthcoming novel *Gertrude Alice Frank*

"Absolutely masterful narrative—the flow, the details, the use of quotations and the presentation of the characters. Robert Dumont's beautiful Natalie Jackson story brings her back to life and reminds us of the turmoil that existed in Beat San Francisco in the mid 1950s with Natalie at its wild beating heart."

JONAH RASKIN
Author of *Beat Blues*

"Robert Dumont gives us a dark rhapsody of scholarly connections in this much needed sleuthing out of the mysterious Natalie Jackson. A lost soul barely scribbled between the lines of the Beats, Kerouac, Ginsberg and Cassady, emerges, flickering. Who was she? Pale ghost of the flaming red hair. We want to know more, and more."

MAUREEN OWEN
Author of *Everything Turns on a Delicate Measure* (Poems)

"Natalie is a cool history of a hot mess. Bob takes a Beat tragedy and tells it for today. You know the players, you know the outcome, it's impossible to look away."

BENITO VILA
Editor of *Charles Plymell's Of Myth & Men* and *Keyboard Intercourse*

AUTHOR'S NOTE

THIS BRIEF BOOK is not a reconstruction of the story of Natalie Jackson's life and death recounted in conventional narrative fashion, nor does it shape her story into a novelistic account that neatly unfolds. Rather, it is assembled through memories, voices, perspectives, and images—a polyphonic method resulting in a layered composition that evokes rather than dictates: a literary collage.

The story of Natalie Jackson as it exists in popular memory and written accounts is already a type of collage that is scattered across memoirs, novels, police archives, and cultural histories. Here some of those pieces are gathered and juxtaposed, revealing tensions, echoes, and silences in the chronicle of her life and death.

By nature, a collage resists resolution. It does not claim to provide a singular truth but rather presents overlapping realities, each shaped by the biases, emotions, and limitations of those who have told and retold Natalie's story or were even a part of it. Some of those accounts are sympathetic, others sensationalized, and still other exploitative.

In presenting Natalie's story this way, I invite the reader to experience it as a narrative assembled from disparate elements, including gaps and juxtapositions that are intentional; a life (and a death) reconstructed after the fact. It is an attempt to hold selected fragments to the light and see what they reveal about Natalie Jackson as a figure in others' stories and at the center of her own.

PART 01

THE SECOND-FLOOR apartment at 1403 Gough Street in San Francisco has a distinctive history behind it, dating back to 1954 when it was occupied by the artist Robert LaVigne. In October of that year, after becoming acquainted with Allen Ginsberg in Foster's Cafeteria, a regular hangout for artists on the ground floor of the Wentley Hotel, LaVigne invited Ginsberg back to his studio to have a look at his paintings.

Ginsberg was working at the time as a market researcher, a job he hated, doing "marketing studies of toiletries [placed] on the front counters of supermarkets," but was relatively flush with cash. He had told LaVigne he might even be interested in purchasing some of his work. Concurrently, Ginsberg was living with a woman named Sheila Boucher, but the relationship was not a congenial one as she objected, among other things, to his continuing attachment to his old friend and former lover Neal Cassady.

Hanging on the wall just outside of LaVigne's Gough Street studio was a large painting called "Nude With Onions" depicting a young man languidly posing on a divan covered with a blanket. (The divan, not the young man, was covered with the blanket.) Ginsberg was immediately taken with the figure in the painting and asked LaVigne who it was.

LaVigne said "Oh, that's Peter. He is here, I'll go get him." Moments later the young man himself walked into the room and Peter Orlovsky met Allen Ginsberg for the first time. The young man greeted him cordially but casually and probably did not notice that the person he was being introduced to was trying not to swoon.

Orlovsky, who had recently been discharged from the Army, was living with LaVigne at the Gough Street apartment.

Also living in one of the rooms in the spacious flat was a tall, slightly gawky, young woman with short-cropped red hair who had been another one of LaVigne's models. Her name was Natalie Jackson and she had arrived in San Francisco from New Jersey some months before. She was working a day job in the J. Magnin Department Store where Marilyn Monroe had bought her wedding dress for her marriage to Joe DiMaggio. By night she was a hipster, a writer, and a "beat muse," a role she had played previously while making the scene in Greenwich Village.

A week or so following his initial visit, Ginsberg paid a return visit to the Gough Street apartment in the company of Neal Cassady. Another one of the paintings LaVigne had hanging in his studio was a nude study of Natalie, and as happened with Ginsberg and the Orlovsky painting, Cassady took one look at it and fell in love with her. Cassady was then living with his wife Carolyn and their three children in Los Gatos and working on the railroad as a conductor. His regular schedule allowed him to ride the commuter train from San Jose to San Francisco in the morning and not return until the evening thus giving him ample time to hang out in the City with his friends on weekdays.

A tense and complicated triangle developed between LaVigne, Ginsberg, and Orlovsky when Ginsberg subsequently moved into the Gough Street apartment. And chaos reigned when Cassady arrived on the premises to see Natalie after his morning train ride in from San Jose. Ginsberg would note in his journal: "Neal rushes in 9 AM—W.C. Fields, Oliver Hardy—pulling on or off his pants, makes it with girl, laughs again, puts on her clothes, she his vest, they blast—and he and I agree on nostalgia of the front door...."

Initially, Ginsberg liked the Gough Street apartment itself. LaVigne had the front room where he worked, and the smell of his oil paints often wafted down the hallway. Peter had a middle room and Natalie was in the back. Cassady was always coming and going and there was a large kitchen where everybody would meet up.

The arrangement between LaVigne, Ginsberg, and Orlovsky proved to be an unstable one, however. Following several heated arguments that Ginsberg called "great magical personality hassles," he moved to a nearby hotel. Gazing out the window from within the darkness of his corner room, Ginsberg would continue to obsess over Peter and hopefully catch a glimpse of him coming and going from Foster's Cafeteria across the street then rush out to "accidentally" bump into him.

LaVigne soon gave up the Gough Street studios and took a room at the Wentley Apartments above Foster's Cafeteria and so did Orlovsky. Meanwhile, the affair between Cassady and Natalie Jackson continued unabated, even after Cassady's wife got wind of it, when he stopped coming home to Los Gatos except on weekends.

In February 1955, Ginsberg convinced Peter to move into a two-bedroom apartment with him at 1010 Montgomery Street in North Beach. LaVigne, realizing he was the odd man out in the new set up, stayed on at the Wentley, but made plans to go to Mexico. With the Gough Street digs now shut down, Natalie and Neal had to find a new place to conduct their love affair. Ginsberg's bed at 1010 Montgomery served the purpose for a while when they weren't jaunting off overnight to L.A. in Neal's Packard. On one occasion he managed to accumulate four speeding tickets along the way.

Eventually, Natalie got an apartment of her own in a three-story building on Franklin Street, only a few blocks from 1403 Gough Street. Ginsberg, who had quit his job as a market researcher and with the two love birds out of the way, was now able to dedicate himself fully to Peter and to writing poetry and working on what would become the opening section of *Howl*.

Allen Ginsberg and Peter Orlovsky would remain lifetime companions from that time forward for the next 42 years, until Ginsberg died, though the relationship was always fraught with personal dramas and difficulties that have been well documented and written about. The hot romance between Natalie Jackson and Neal Cassady had only a matter of months to run however, before it ended suddenly and tragically.

PART 02

THEIR AFFAIR LASTED through much of 1955. Natalie Jackson was present at the famous reading of the first section of Ginsberg's *Howl* on October 7, accompanied by Cassady. In his novel *The Dharma Bums*, Jack Kerouac, using the pseudonym Ray Smith, recreates the scene that evening. "I followed the whole gang of howling poets to the reading at Gallery Six that night, which was, among other things, the night of the birth of the San Francisco Renaissance. Everyone was there. It was a mad night. And I was the one that got things jumping by going around collecting dimes and quarters from the rather stiff audience standing around in the gallery and coming back with three huge gallon jugs of California Burgundy getting them all piffed so that by eleven o'clock when Alvah Goldbrook [*Allen Ginsberg*] was reading his poem "Wail" [*Howl*] drunk with arms outspread everybody was yelling 'Go! Go! Go!' (like at a jam session....")

"Among the people standing in the audience was Rosie Buchanan [Natalie Jackson], a girl with a short haircut, red-haired, bony, handsome, a real gone chick and friend of everybody of any consequence on the Beach, who'd been a painter's model and a writer herself and was bubbling over with excitement at the time because she was in love with my old buddy Cody Pomeroy [Neal Cassady]. 'Great, hey Rosie?' I yelled and she took a big slug from my jug and shined eyes at me. Cody just stood there behind her with both arms around her waist."

Afterwards, Kerouac and his crew piled into cars and drove to the *Nam Yuen* which was a favorite venue in Chinatown of Gary Snyder, one of the evening's other readers, "for a big fabulous dinner off the Chinese menu, with chopsticks, yelling conversation in the middle of the night in one of those great free-swinging Chinese restaurants in

San Francisco."

For Natalie, it must have been an extraordinary night as well. No worries about her job at the department store—tomorrow she'd put on a plaid skirt and a white sweater, take a bennie, and get through the work day—with many thoughts of just how far she'd come from her former life in East Orange. All behind her was her family—a father who liked to play the ponies, an older sister Rita living in Florida whose husband was tied-in with the mob—and her own nowhere job as a cashier at the Kresge's store in Newark.

Behind her as well was the unwanted child she had put up for adoption and a half-hearted suicide attempt in New York. She had found her soul mate in Neal and the photo that Allen had taken of them on Market Street under the movie marquis for *The Wild One* with Marlon Brando seemed appropriate, as if she was starring in her own version of a film with that same title, and that moment captured in the photograph was like a movie still from it.

After the Chinese food and some foolish banter with the cook at *Nam Yuen* who had replied, "I don't care," when asked a question about Buddhism, as if he should know, (which was deemed as the perfect Zen answer by Snyder), the gang of poets once again piled into cars and split for The Place, a bar and gallery in North Beach and one of their regular haunts.

The conversation would be lively between the "howling" and now yacking poets who were still on a high from the excitement of the reading earlier in the evening. Among this group, Natalie could easily hold her own. She was one of those characters that Kerouac would describe in *On the Road* who "burn, burn, burn, like fabulous yellow roman candles exploding… across the stars."

Burning brightly indeed but the darkness was inexorably approaching.

PART 03

SHORTLY AFTER THE night of the reading at Gallery Six, Neal Cassady, hatched a scheme in which he convinced Natalie to pose as his wife, Carolyn, and forge her signature in order to withdraw the sum of ten-thousand dollars from Carolyn's investment account. With the money in hand Cassady went to the Bay Meadows Race Track in San Mateo over the course of several days to employ a "fail-proof" system of gambling on the horses which he had learned from Natalie, who'd probably learned it from her father. It involved betting at the last minute on the third-ranked horse, in any given race, an amount that would cover any previous losses. The "fail-proof" system wasn't, and Neal soon managed to lose the entire $10,000.

Though Carolyn Cassady chose not to prosecute after being informed by the bank of what had happened to her money, Natalie became convinced that the police would soon be coming after her and all of Neal's Beat cohorts. She obsessively binged on amphetamines and began cutting herself. Neal had already decided his girlfriend was crazy and was at a loss at what to do about her. Ginsberg was no help. While Peter was in New York dealing with a family crisis, he had decamped from Montgomery Street and moved across the Bay to Berkeley where he was holed up in a cottage and now working on later sections of *Howl*.

He would see Natalie one last time when she came to his place to spend Thanksgiving. He thought she appeared to be troubled and observed that she was "tearful." But he was in no position to be her therapist, nor interested in doing so. Previously, on Montgomery Street, he had mentioned in a letter to Kerouac that after one of her love-making sessions with Cassady she "keeps hanging around to talk to me[.] I can't stand it (tho she's a hip redhead frantic lost days), but I'm too weak to listen to lost talk…."

Al Hinkle, a member of the North Beach scene urged Cassady to have Natalie admitted to a hospital after she had slashed her wrists with a dull knife. But Neal thought she'd be okay if he or somebody else were able to keep an eye on her for a few days.

On the afternoon of November 30, Neal asked Jack to look after Natalie for the evening while he was at work. Kerouac had come into San Francisco from Berkeley where he was staying and was intent on "having fun" while hanging out at The Place that night, but acceded to Neal's request. He went over to a nearby cafeteria on Van Ness Street and got some sandwiches for he and Natalie to eat for dinner.

Once again, in *The Dharma Bums*, Kerouac describes his encounter with Natalie on what she had said was going to be the last night of her life. "I went over to Rosie's place… and tried to make her eat. She sat in the kitchen staring at me… I was amazed to see her, she'd changed so suddenly, she was…skinny and a skeleton and her eyes were huge with terror and popping out of her face." Later in the evening she was standing "in the kitchen of the little apartment with her skeletal hands held out in supplicatory explanation, her legs braced, her red hair all frizzly, trembling and shuddering and grabbing her face from time to time."

Natalie was stating adamantly, "The police are going to swoop down and arrest us all and… we're going to be questioned for weeks and weeks and maybe years until they find out *all* the crimes and sins that have been committed… finally they'll arrest everybody in North Beach and even everybody in Greenwich Village and then Paris and then finally they'll have *everybody* in jail…."

This accorded with what Neal had told Kerouac earlier about an incident at her work at the department store. He said that Natalie told him she had written down the names of all her friends and listed their sins then attempted to flush the pages down the toilet. The toilet backed up and overflowed and a sanitation attendant in a uniform then arrived to unstop the toilet and clean up the mess. Natalie was convinced the attendant was a cop and had taken the list of names back to the police station.

"She's just nuts, that's all," was Cassady's assessment.

Kerouac responded to Natalie by telling

her that this business with the cops was all "bullshit" and then felt frustrated the same as he did whenever he tried to explain Buddhism to friends and family members who weren't already enlightened, or interested in the topic.

He insisted that she shut up and listen to him: "You're getting these silly convictions and conceptions out of nowhere; don't you realize all this life is just a dream? Why don't you just relax and enjoy God. God is *you*; you fool!"

Kerouac's bedside manner and Buddhist maxims were not having their intended effect. Natalie roared back at him: "Oh they're going to destroy you [Jack], I can see it, they're going to fetch all the religious squares and fix them good. It's only just begun. It's all tied in with Russia… and something I heard about the sun's rays and about something that happens when we're all asleep. Oh [Jack] the world will never be the same!"

"What world? What difference does it make?" was Kerouac's only retort. He finally gave up and declared, "I won't listen to another word." He then left the apartment to buy some wine and met up with a group of jazz musicians who lived in the building's basement. He invited them all upstairs so the whole gang returned to Natalie's apartment where Kerouac told her to "have some wine, put some wisdom in your head." The joys of the cup now apparently supplanting the wisdom of the Buddha.

Natalie, still having no use for Kerouac's platitudes, stated that she was "laying off the lush, all that wine you drink is rotgut, it burns your stomach out, it makes your brain dull… you're not sensitive, you don't *realize* what's going on."

"Oh come on."

"This is my last night on earth," she added ominously.

Kerouac and the musicians drank the wine and talked until around midnight. Natalie finally appeared to have calmed down somewhat. She lay down on the couch, even laughed at some of the remarks between Kerouac and the musicians. He brewed her a cup of tea and she nibbled at one of the sandwiches he'd purchased on Van Ness Street. After the musicians left, Kerouac unrolled his sleeping bag and dozed off on the kitchen floor until Neal returned, at which point he split, presumably for The Place, to catch up with the North Beach gang.

While Cassady slept in the bedroom Natalie made her way to the roof of the 3-story building wearing only a T-shirt under a bathrobe. She broke a skylight and slashed her wrists and cut her throat then sat there bleeding until dawn when a neighbor saw her. The neighbor alerted her husband who called the police.

With the approaching sirens, Natalie must have believed all that she had foreseen was coming to pass. The police were now coming for her and would be rounding up everybody she knew and was associated with. She moved back and forth between her own building and the roof of an adjoining building as the sirens were closing in. She could not get away. There was nowhere else to go. And she was alone. Where were Jack and Neal and the musicians who had visited her apartment earlier?

Probably they had already been apprehended. And the cops were coming for her. There was one on the street below shouting something at her. She moved onto the building's fire escape and stood poised outside its railing. Where could she go? Suddenly, a window looking onto the fire escape was thrown open and here was another cop lunging towards her and grabbing a hold of her bathrobe and her arm. They thought they had apprehended her. But they hadn't. She pulled her arm away. She felt the bathrobe fall from her shoulders and from her body. And then she felt like she was flying. It was a miracle. The cops would never capture her or be able to interrogate her now.

She would be one of the lucky ones.

At this very moment, Kerouac was with his friends he had met up with at The Place "having fun." He'd done all he could do for Natalie as a favor to Neal. What else was he supposed to do?

And Neal was asleep in the apartment though he had been disturbed by the sound of the approaching sirens.

The jazz musicians were back in their basement apartment playing records and still talking endlessly. The day was dawning, and they would eventually need to get some sleep as they had a gig to play that night. But the sirens that had at first been distant were now on their block, and then were right outside their door. They heard somebody shouting outside on the sidewalk in front of their building. There was a thud as something hit the sidewalk and even more commotion. More sirens. More shouts. They stayed inside their apartment but kept peeking out the basement windows at the "horrible sight" until they could

stand it no more. They closed the curtains.
    Then decided to cancel their gig that night.

SAN FRANCISCO CHRONICLE, Thursday, Dec. 1, 1955

Woman Fights Off Rescue, Leaps 3 Stories to Death

Out of Sight, Out of Money, Widow Finds

This is 1041 Franklin street, where an unidentified young woman leaped to her death yesterday - dotted lines [show path]

Gas Price War in East Bay

usade Reports 748,948— 8% of Goal

Fifth Fugitive From Preston Surrenders

PART 04

SLIGHTLY MORE THAN twenty-four hours later in Los Gatos, Carolyn Cassady sent her kids off to school then, as was her morning ritual, sat and drank a cup of coffee and read the *San Francisco Chronicle* while she had a few moments to herself. On page 2 she was drawn to a headline and an accompanying photo that normally would not have interested her. The headline read WOMAN FIGHTS OFF RESCUE, LEAPS 3 STORIES TO DEATH.

The photo showed a typical three-story San Francisco-style Victorian house on Franklin Street, its front rising in twin rounded turret-style window bays stacked one atop the other with a wrought-iron fire escape descending between them. At the top left, a domed cupola gave the roofline a certain elegance, while the right side ended in a blunt, square projection that seemed to cut off the symmetry. The street-level entrance, set deep into the building's lower right, looked more like a shadowed alcove than a doorway. A superimposed dotted line ran from the roof to the sidewalk depicting the path of the woman's fall. The dotted line ended next to a parked car on the street. A Packard. Her hands began to tremble as she read the text of the article.

"An unidentified woman about 35 years old slashed her throat on a roof top at 1041 Franklin Street yesterday, then kicked free from the grip of a husky policeman and jumped to her death from a third-story fire escape.

Wearing only a bathrobe and a T-shirt, she stood poised outside the railing of the narrow fire escape walkway as Officer O'Rourke lunged through a window to grab her. "All I could do was dive through and grab," he said.

"I got a grip on one arm and her robe just as she tried to kick loose. But I couldn't hold her. All at

once I was just holding the robe, and she had fallen. His partner said she might have slashed herself with fragments from a broken skylight."

Officer O'Rourke's partner, Officer Dick Rader, told the author of the *Chronicle* article, that he had spotted the unknown woman on the roof of the house and had shouted up to her, "No, no, no!" while his partner raced to the top floor.

Carolyn tried to talk herself out of fearing the worst, of over-dramatizing things. It could have been anyone's Packard parked there in front of the building, and besides, the article had stated the dead woman was 35 and had blonde hair. She knew that this Natalie girl friend of Neal's was several years younger and was not a blonde.

Note: The address given in the Chronicle article — 1041 Franklin — was incorrect. Later reporting identified the correct location as 1045.

Neal Cassady and Natalie Jackson conscious of their roles in Eternity, Market Street San Francisco 1955. As prototype of hero in Jack Kerouac's late 1940's Saga On the Road (Dean Moriarty), Cassady's illuminated American automobile enthusiasm and erotic energy had already written his name in bright lights of our literary imagination before movies were able imitating his original charm. That's why we stopped under the marquee to fix the passing hand on the diamond watch. Allen Ginsberg.

PART 05

CAROLYN HAD NEVER met her in person but several months before when she was with Neal in San Francisco, they had gone to visit the artist Bob LaVigne at his 1403 Gough St. apartment. LaVigne, at the time, was working on a large mural with a red-haired seated nude in the center whose name was Natalie Jackson.

Not long afterwards, Neal began acting secretive and spending more time away from home. About the only "reliable" time they had together was on weekends. She was not to learn exactly what was going on until she had been going through the pockets of Neal's jeans preparing to wash them and she came across two letters and some notes written between Neal and Natalie, as well as photos of the two of them, no doubt taken by Allen, "cavorting" on the streets of San Francisco. One of them depicted them embracing in front of a movie theater on Market Street beneath a marquee that advertised Marlon Brando in *The Wild One*.

There were other photos of Neal and Natalie, and the young woman didn't strike Carolyn as being particularly attractive—was somewhat androgynous and awkward in appearance.

She later heard from their friends Al and Helen Hinkle who had met Natalie a couple of times that she was "weird" and appeared to be catatonic and often stared into space. Carolyn didn't get why Neal would be so enamored of her, but Al Hinkle said that Natalie was known around North Beach for "certain oral sexual practices" so that made it more understandable on the surface. But the tone of the letters Carolyn had found gave evidence of a more serious relationship.

After confronting him and then some half-hearted attempts at reconciliation, employing prayer and meditation and reading books that elucidated the teachings of Edgar Cayce, Neal had announced that he was moving into San Francisco to share an apartment with Allen and Peter because it would be more convenient for his work.

"Allen and Peter, my foot… [it's] Natalie!" was Carolyn's reaction.

Still in the Caycean mode, she opted for "long suffering" over divorce. Only if God so willed it would their separation be permanent. She consoled herself with such Caycean maxims as "If you want to be loved, be lovely"; and "Love is like a mirror—the more given out, the more is reflected back, and thus it expands"; and "Let go and let God."

These precepts were more for self-inspiration and morale-building, but she practiced them even more enthusiastically, when onto the scene and into the middle of the Natalie imbroglio came Jack Kerouac and the two of them were able to re-kindle their long-smoldering romance.

And Neal would still turn up in Los Gatos every couple of weeks on pay-days and on at least one occasion Carolyn and Jack had accompanied him to Bay Meadows Raceway. She'd never known Neal to be an aficionado of horse racing and he kept touting a cockamamie system of betting that he swore was scientific but resulted in no winnings on that particular day.

She didn't think to ask where the money was coming from that Neal was using to cover his bets. She just followed the advice of Edgar Cayce and Jack, as far as Neal was concerned, to "let go and let God."

That is, until one day when Jack went off with Neal and she received a call from the bank informing her that she needed to return because when she and her husband had been in the other day to withdraw all the money, there was one more piece of paper that needed to be signed in order to close the account.

Her mind went blank. She laughed nervously. "Oh, you must have the wrong Cassady. I haven't been in your bank since last year." The person from the bank asked if they were no longer planning to move back East because her mother had died. The story became more preposterous. But the money was gone. $10,000 squandered on Neal's betting system. She didn't even bother to confront him. Just wrote him a note letting him know she knew the whole story then lay in bed most of the night by herself gritting her teeth and repeating every charitable Christian principle she could recall:

"Bless those who despitefully use you." "Resist not evil." "Judge not that ye be not judged." "Love your enemies." "Vengeance is mine saith the Lord."

She further rationalized that it was Neal's money and not hers because they had received it as a settlement for an injury he'd sustained while working on the railway. At least they still had the house.

Ever willing to cut him all the slack in the world, Carolyn believed that Neal would be overcome with guilt and contrition the day after leaving him the note. And he seemingly was. He said he had been sure that the system was going to work, that he would strike it rich, and they'd be set for life. But instead of following the system he explained, he'd tried to take short cuts by listening to touts and tipsters and playing the long odds. The concept was correct, it was just the execution of it that had caused him to piss away $10,000 over the course of the past month.

She savored now having the upper hand with him. "Neal, what dumbfounds me… is that you always manage to get caught… Do you suppose subconsciously you demand to be punished? You're always dropping clues about for me to find, like Natalie's notes. I don't even have to be a nosy wife."

"It sure looks that way," he had responded weakly.

"Well I don't want to punish you. Get somebody else to be your warden or mother—go to confession. It's a role I detest...."

Carolyn "didn't give up the role overnight" but felt some relief and validation as her behavior improved. She and Neal were actually getting along better, their relationship was more "workable"; they could discuss things "objectively, even lovingly, instead of throwing up a wall of emotions between us and battering it uselessly."

Drawing on the Caycean precepts she had arrived at the following conclusion: "We often skirted the crater of despair, but with our growing knowledge of life's principles and purpose there was a place to turn to, a direction to follow, and we'd already learned that when we managed to act on the *theory*, it never failed to work."

PART 06

AT ANY RATE, there was no reason to be apprehensive she told herself as she continued drinking her coffee and reading the rest of the paper. Nevertheless, she could not get the dotted line between the roof of the house and the sidewalk out of her mind. And the Packard parked in the street. The same type of car that Neal drove.

One hour later Neal phoned her. "Carolyn… Natalie… is dead."

"I saw the paper, Neal. I'm so sorry. Do you want to come home for a while?"

"Oh could I?"

"Of course, Neal. This is your home still… [!] I know you loved her. It must be awful for you."

Recalling this scene years later while writing her own book, *Off the Road – My Years With Cassady, Kerouac, and Ginsberg,* Carolyn Cassady chose not to characterize or depict her own state of mind.

That evening Neal arrived at the Los Gatos house "looking gray and gaunt." His wife thought that she'd "never seen him so unhinged and defenseless."

She made him some coffee and sensed he wanted to speak but was hesitant. She tried to make it easy for him.

"I saw your car in the photograph. Where were you?"

Where he was and what he was doing was sleeping in the bedroom until the sirens had awakened him. He saw that Natalie was gone and knew something was up. He told his wife, "I thought of you and the kids getting involved and just grabbed my stuff and ran out the back way."

"I certainly thank you for that." Though she "hated" to raise the topic of suicide she went ahead anyway, knowing that Neal, convinced by their readings of Cayce, believed that suicide was the ultimate offense against oneself and against God.

"Neal groaned. 'I don't know...I don't want to believe that—but she had become completely paranoid the past couple of weeks. She had an obsession about cops. Part of it was feeling so guilty about forging your signature—she has been agonizing ever since—and she did that for me....."

He said he tried to tell Natalie that his wife was not angry, that she'd gone to the bank and re-signed the papers okaying the withdrawal, but Natalie wouldn't listen. She obsessed over her sin and her guilt and was convinced she would be arrested. She tried to cut herself with a dull knife and Neal talked to her about suicide and told her not to think of harming herself again.

"I thought she was better—in fact, she was her old self last night and we'd talked a long time. I'll never know if she really cut her throat on purpose. One paper said she fell on the skylight... and she didn't actually *jump*—she was so afraid of the cop, when he grabbed for her she must have backed up and [fallen] off...."

Even in this dire circumstance Carolyn evoked the *theory*. She consoled him with the idea that "maybe it was an out for her.... Maybe it was a chance for Natalie to change her course—[to]

start over. She seemed to have boxed herself in. It could be a merciful release, couldn't it?"

Neal allowed himself to be soothed by Carolyn's Caycean bromides. "Yeah, I suppose it really is better for her. She was insane—I couldn't help her."

PART 07

JACK KEROUAC, or Ray Smith, the character he had created of himself in *The Dharma Bums*, upon reading the newspaper and seeing the dotted line tracing the path of the fall of the unknown woman from the roof of 1045 Franklin Street, to the sidewalk next to Neal's car, thought to himself, "If only she'd listened to me… Was I talking so dumb after all? Are my ideas about what to do so silly and stupid and childlike? Isn't this the time now to start following what I know to be true?"

It's unclear who was to do the following. Kerouac? Or the rest of the world? It was a theory similar to the one that Carolyn adhered to that "never fails to work." In the end Kerouac decided it was best to lay low and not get further involved, especially with the police.

The following day Neal returned to the apartment and got the rest of his things and brought them back to Los Gatos. The papers were reporting that the body of the woman who died in the fall remained unidentified—was still a "Jane Doe."

Initially, the manager of the building at 1045 Franklin had been on the scene but subsequently was nowhere to be found. The coroner determined that the woman's skull had been was fractured and she also suffered a contusion. The official cause of death was "multiple traumatic injuries." The coroner noted in the autopsy report that "There was no means of identification found on the deceased person and no one in the vicinity could identify the deceased." He further noted there was no evidence of alcohol or drugs in her system.

Neal and Carolyn decided it would be safe for him to go to the police and provide them with a name and "get the poor girl settled." Before doing so Neal also consulted with his first wife LuAnne. He told her that Natalie's death was a "punishment" or at least a "warning." The police report would later state that the dead woman was identified by a "friend." Some days later, Irene Jackson arrived from New Jersey to claim her daughter's body.

Carolyn Cassady, for her part, felt that "God had made a separation," whatever that meant, and "resolved to work even harder to make Neal happy, now that this obstacle had been removed."

Cold words for a cold world.

PART 08

ON THE 11TH OF December, following a poetry reading by Kenneth Rexroth, a sort of impromptu memorial remembrance of Natalie took place. On hand were Allen Ginsberg, Jack Kerouac, Gary Snyder, Philip Whalen, Robert LaVigne, and a few others who had known Natalie. Later, LaVigne would do a sketch he entitled "Dirge for Natalie Jackson."

Kerouac had now decided to depart from "that city of ignorance" he considered San Francisco and all modern cities to be. He spent a few dreary, rainy days with Neal and Carolyn in

Los Gatos. Neal was sad and praying for Natalie because he believed her death was a suicide, therefore it was an open question whether her soul was bound for hell or for purgatory.

In *The Dharma Bums* the character Cody Pomeroy declares, "We've got to get her to purgatory, man." Ray Smith then says, "So I helped him pray…."

During the short time Kerouac was there, Carolyn Cassady observed that Neal's obsession with the horse race betting system increased as if he were atoning for having lost their savings and for Natalie. He spent an hour every evening pouring over the race results and making his calculations. If he did bet, the sums were not of a sufficient amount to make or break the family finances.

After hopping on board a freight bound for L.A., the Kerouac character reflects on things: "Poor Rosie [Natalie]—she had been absolutely *certain* that the world was real and fear was real and now what was real? At least… she's in heaven, and she knows."

Later, beside a small campfire near Riverside, he is in his sleeping bag and about to embark in the morning on a 3,000-mile hitchhike back to his mother's house in North Carolina. Under the stars he says a prayer for…[Natalie]: "If she'd lived, and could have come here with me, maybe I could have told her something, made her feel different. Maybe I'd just make love to her and say nothing."

Natalie Jackson, San Francisco 1955.   Allen Ginsberg

CODA

ALLEN GINSBERG would process the death of Natalie Jackson in his own way, also by writing about her. It was to be in an untitled poem from his journal written in 1956:

> *Already Time for your elegy, dear Natalie?*
> *Already time for your angelic shock?*
> *Already your blood meaningless,*
> *   and your untruthful eyes*
> *   troubling me too late?*
> *Should I have invited you to Berkeley?*
> *Given you money? Or more love?*

or a rest home in my lovely crazy garden?
In the car over for Thanksgiving
you gave me a look so tearful
I knew it was death
or thought so
and it passed my mind
not my time yet
I ignored you.
I closed my light lay back
& try to pray for you
Take refuge in my prayer
Take refuge in Pater Omnipotens Aeterne Deus
Take refuge in Love (which is God)
Self-Love
Oh, Natalie, where is refuge?
Take refuge in Death.
Finally, it is death I wish—
not the horror blood be-dabbled knees
and ankles on a pavement
or a throat cut by electric bulbs—
Dark death, Soft death
Black eternal grave
and rest.

FROM THE LENS OF ALLEN GINSBERG

Photographs by Allen Ginsberg with captions transcribed from his original handwritten notes—offering a candid glimpse into the Beat Generation's inner circle.

Cover Photograph:
Peter Du Peru, Neal Cassady & Natalie Jackson horsing around, maybe Sunday walk, above Broadway tunnell, (sic). Neal playing hooky from his family in Los Gatos. Du Peru, eccentric North Beach remittance man was seen by Kerouac (Desolation Angels) as "Richard de Chili, the Mysterious…with his low-spoken incomprehensible remarks." Natalie, bewildered by amphetamine jumped off her roof to death a year later. March 1955, San Francisco.
—Allen Ginsberg

Interior Photograph (p. 12):
Natalie Jackson and Neal Cassady, car lot.

Interior Photograph (p. 26):
Neal Cassady and Natalie Jackson conscious of their roles in Eternity, Market Street San Francisco 1955. As prototype of hero in Jack Kerouac's late 1940s saga <u>On the Road</u> (Dean Moriarity), Cassady's illuminated automobile enthusiasm and erotic energy had already written his name in bright lights of our literary imagination before movies were made imitating his original charm. That's why we stopped under the marquee to fix the passing hand on the diamond watch.
—Allen Ginsberg

Interior Photograph (p. 44):
Natalie Jackson, San Francisco 1955. —Allen Ginsberg

BIBLIOGRAPHY

Kerouac, Jack: *The Dharma Bums*. (novel) Viking Press 1958.

Cassady, Carolyn: *Off the Road: My Years with Cassady, Kerouac, and Ginsberg*. William Morrow 1990; *Heart Beat - My Life with Jack and Neal*. (autobiography) Creative Arts Press 1976.

Cassady, Neal: *Collected Letters* 1944-1967. Penguin Books 1991.

Morgan, Bill: *The Beat Generation in San Francisco: A Literary Tour*. City Lights Books 2003.

Schwartz, Mark & Peterson, Art: "The Place - Historical Essay;" *The Semaphore* #181, Fall 2007.

Juska, Jane "Another View of The Place: I Was There," 2007. *Found SF-The San Francisco Digital History*.

Segal, Deborah C. *Natalie's Story - A Raincheck for Jack Kerouac* (Play) Mel C.Thompson Publishing Company 2011

Raskin, Jonah: *Beat Blues*: San Francisco, 1955 (novel) Coolgrove Press 2021; "The Wild Ones: Natalie Jackson (1931-1955) & the Usual Suspects—Neal Cassady, Jack Kerouac, Allen Ginsberg & Peter Orlovsky." *Counter Culture Magazine* 2014.

Dale, Rick: "Remembering Natalie Jackson." *The Daily Beat* 11-30-2021.

Wills, David: "Beat and Damned: the Death of Natalie Jackson; an essay..." Substack 2024.

ABOUT THE AUTHOR

Robert Dumont is an Oklahoma native and a graduate of Tulsa University. He is the author of the short story collection: *Borough of Churches* and a collage-novel: *NYC Transit[s]*. He is a co-editor (with Astra Beck and Dion Wright) of *State Line-Collected Poems and Other Writings* by Alan Russo (Rosace Publications).

He currently lives in Brooklyn, NY.

BOOKS BROUGHT OUT BY ROSACE PUBLICATIONS

ANTHOLOGIES
Smoking Mirror (1974) Chapbook
Le Feu Du Ciel (1965) Chapbook

BY DAVID OMER BEARDEN
The Thing in Packy Innard's Place (2019) Novel
The Mental Traveler (2018) Poems
Redress (1983) Chapbook
The Rosace in a Star Chamber (1981) Chapbook
So Long at the Fair & Down at the Palomino Club & Other Poems (1976) Chapbook

BY ALAN BÄTJER RUSSO
State Line (2021) Collected Poems and Other Writings
DOMINION and Other Poems (1977) Chapbook

BY DION WRIGHT
Zip Area (Forthcoming) Correspondence Collection
Tempus Fugitive (2016) Memoir of the 60s

BY ROBERT DUMONT
Natalie (2025) Biographical Collage

LEARN MORE AT
ROSACEPUBLICATIONS.COM

www.ingramcontent.com/pod-product-compliance
Lightning Source LLC
Chambersburg PA
CBHW061235070526
44584CB00030B/4130